Mustard Seeds

Mustard Seeds

A Collection of Poems

TRINA FRANCIS

Genesis Publishing

FIRST EDITION

ISBN 978-1-09836-086-3

Printed in the United States of America.

For Lou Lou,

you are not here to see the manifestation of this dream,

but you were certainly a major contributor.

Rest in Heaven Mama
Laura Lou Francis
1942 - 2017

To my children who give me a reason to get out of bed.

To my GrandShuga, Layla, that fills my heart with love, even as she claims it all.

To my sisters (none of which are biological) for pushing me

when I was too afraid to move forward,

for lifting me when I was down,

for guiding me when I was uncertain, and

for showing me parts of myself that I didn't see.

CONTENTS

Just Let Me Breathe

George Floyd 2020

Why are you so threatened
By the color of my skin
Yes I have more melanin
But we're both the same within

If you cut me
Will I not bleed
If you threaten me
Will I not plead

The blood of Jesus covers me
Does it not cover you
That question is rhetorical
There's no answer for what you do

Tell me, what color is your heart
I can only assume that it's black
Mine is purple and blue
Because of the oxygen that it lacks

I only desire to live my life
The way that God ordained
But somehow you can't live in peace
Unless l am bound and chained

But lately that isn't even enough
To set your spirit right
So you dress up as policemen
To justify taking my life

1

Why are you so threatened
By the color of my skin
Yes I have more melanin
But we're both the same within

When I run
Do I not sweat
When I bathe
Am I not wet

How can you hate me so much
That you can look into my eyes
And take away my last breath
Based on Karen's lies

Why do you hate my father
My brother, my nephew, my son
I'm so tired of hurting
From all the damage you've done

Lord I ask you now
To reign down on this earth
Help us to live the lives
That you intended from our birth

Let no weapon formed against us
Land where it's intended
Wherever there's a broken heart
I pray that you would mend it

I'm not asking that evil befall anyone
That's not something I need
My prayer is for peaceful coexistence
My plea is "Just Let Me Breathe"

Phenomenal Woman

I am a Phenomenal Woman
Maya said it best
There are characteristics within me so profound
They can't be contained by flesh

When I see my reflection in the mirror
I see a pretty face for sure
But my eyes penetrate the surface
To see all God created me for

I am a screw up, Oh, you noticed
Here, let me applaud
But that means nothing, because like Mary Jane
I am beautifully flawed

I don't base my self-worth
On the things that you perceive
Because at the end of the day, it's not about what you think
It's about what I choose to believe

And I know who I am and whose I am
So even if I am worthless in your mind
That doesn't make me less of a diamond
It just means you share less of my shine

The exclamation of this reality
Is not bred from arrogant pride
But rather from a desperate need
To help nourish my people from the inside

Little flakes of negativity
Are constantly fed into our brains
But I challenge you to milk your soul with affirmation
Of the positive that remains
And stop sabotaging your relationships
Simply because you are afraid
Remember, brothers and sisters
You were fearfully and wonderfully made

Let me share with you
The quickest way to get on our Savior's nerve
Keep telling him and telling yourself
What it is you feel you don't deserve

We are Kings and Queens, heirs to the throne
Descendants of royalty
Though sticks and stones may break our bones
Our faith will set us free

My faith in God reminds me daily
That I was sent to this earth as a gift
Because of situations I needed to help cast down
And spirits I needed to help uplift

Yet even as God shaped me
In the palms of His mighty hands
He knew that the vessel He formed
Would still be just a man

So imperfections, my Father knew
Were sure to be common place
But He already had a plan for blood
To cover His creation with Grace

So I have learned to see myself as God sees me
And to love myself beyond measure
Because if God sees me as priceless
Who am I to question His treasure

I am phenomenal because I am His
And you are phenomenal too
God made me incredibly different
Just like He made an incredible you

Love's Taken Over

When I saw him, it was our eyes that did the honor of the introductions
His pupils danced as they offered me the entrance into his soul
I found love there
But it was bound and gagged as if kidnapped
Yet made no attempts to be free

But I knew
I knew that my love could reach his lowest lows
And coerce them into his highest highs
But why, why risk the health of my heart you ask
But are not all journeys unsure
Are there not consequences to all love

Hmph! I remember the very day our love was born
It was a difficult delivery
Unsure of the future, he was reluctant to push through the pain to the possibility
But in the end, passion and promise prevailed
And he and I together gave birth to a beautiful new love

And now, He loves me
He makes me feel like leaves that are warmed by the sun
And encouraged by the wind to dance
Even the birds know why I glow!
In his presence my body becomes voice-activated
Responding to his every command
How does he do it

Just by being him

The radiance he pours into me seeps through my skin
Until my cocoa covering turns golden bronze
He is sweet like the sugar in my cornbread
Yet rugged like the saddle that convinces me that it's okay to ride
And what a wonderful ride it is!
I plan to ride it until the wheels fall off!

He loves me!
There are days when I think to myself
I wonder if as a child, he had trouble spelling the word "man"
Because today, he clearly defines it
Like *Coke*, he is the real thing! And I love him
It is thoughts of him that motivate my heart to beat
And encourage my breath to run laps around my respiratory system

Pray for me ya'll!
Pray for me because only the feet of Jesus
Will be sufficient enough to overcome the footprints
That this man's love will leave behind

I know that I will always love him
No matter where he is
Here or there, near or far, rich or poor, sick or in health
I will love him til the day I die
And when I'm gone
I will send him angel kisses from the sky

To describe our love
I guess not enough vocabulary exists or is simply hard to choose
So, to make a long story a little shorter
Let me sum it all up by simply saying
My man is my muse
And love has taken over

The Essence of a Queen

I have a dream of a prosperous life
Having a career, being a mother and wife
I have the brains, the courage, and the skills
To capture my dreams as it is God's will
I possess gifts that you have not seen
I am the essence of an African Queen

You think you can hold me back because I am a woman
Darker than a paper sack
As sure as I stand I say to you
You will never hold me back
I will stand tall and reach out for my dreams
I am the essence of an African Queen

I love who I am now and who I strive to become
Growing by leaps and bounds with one foot on where I'm from
For there lies the foundation on which I was raised
Thinking about it still leaves me amazed
Folks that I labeled as harsh and as mean
Were just molding my life as an African Queen

My ancestors slaved through day and through night
Fighting oppression with only their lives
They climbed the mountains we simply pass through
Just one thing they accomplished for me and for you
To them I say don't fret your toils were not in vain
The victory of your struggle still remains
Even in the midst of violence it's not as hopeless as it seems
Because of you, I am the essence of an African Queen

Nature of a Brother

Shades of Perfection
Vanilla, Banana, Caramel, Cocoa, and Charcoal
Hair so straight, so curly, so wavy
An afro, braids, and even the dreads
The eyes, oh yes, magnificent eyes
Tell the secrets the heart desires to hide
Mmmm! The scents, such wonderful scents
The evidence of a day's work
The hint of a recent shower
The rapture of body chemistry
With just a touch
Of favored cologne
Fingers, hands, arms of strength
Legs of endurance
A sensitive, yeah, oh yeah, a sensitive heart
The very nature of intelligence
To build a whole nation
Yet never receive due props
But faith
Faith in God enables
Stand tall, stand proud, stand firm
Your Queen she stands
She always stands right beside you

Acknowledge Me

Excuse me fellas
May I have your attention
There's just a couple of things
That I'd like to mention

Yes, I know, you don't know me
And I'm not your neighbor
But still I'd really like
To ask you a favor

You see I realize
That I'm thick in the thighs
And I'm not a size 2
So, I'm no good for you

But all I'm asking is that you acknowledge me

Don't walk up to girls in a pack
And only acknowledge
The one that attracts
You, because you feel
The rest of us lack
What it takes to get the attention of your mack

All I'm asking is that you acknowledge me

Don't hold the door for your girl
To enter a place
But then let it go
To close in my face

I know I'm not
The best-looking woman you've ever seen
But that doesn't make me
Any less of a Queen

All I'm asking is that you acknowledge me

I'm not asking for your hand in marriage
Or even that you help me push a baby carriage
I realize that you don't like what you see
And to be honest, you're not that attractive to me

All I'm asking is for you to acknowledge me

Truth be told if I gave you a week
You couldn't find what I lack
Instead, you'd be on the phone calling your girl
Saying, "Baby, I'm not coming back!"

But don't worry sugar, you're going back
Cuz I'm not trying to ruin your life
Since I am obviously too much woman for you
Go ahead, make that skinny heffa your wife

All I'm asking you to do is acknowledge me

You see I realize that there are still some good men out there
Though like needles in a haystack
That can appreciate a good woman like me
Cause he knows I'll have his back

And someday when God is ready
That special man will make me his wife
And I promise you
That man is in for the ride of his life

You know what, on second thought
I don't need you to acknowledge me

But the next time you see a woman
That's too short or too tall
Too big or too small
Oddly shaped or lacking this kind of curves
Promise me that you'll acknowledge *her*

For You

My greatest desire
Is to hold you
And be held by you
To look into your eyes
And see the same love
That I feel leaving my heart
Each time you dance around my mind
Your taste
Your smell
Your touch
Each takes its turn
Wreaking havoc on my soul
Whenever you're not with me
My only solace
Kenny's voice reminding me that
Everything I'm feeling
Everything I do, my love
It's all for you
Please know that no matter what
However long I have to wait
All my love is for you

Salvation is Free

I often wonder
What I ever did to deserve you
And then I remember

Salvation is free

God sent Jesus to save my life
He sent you
To save my heart

Wildflower

I am buried under the dirt of being dark
In a world that prefers light

I am buried under the dirt of being a black woman
In a world that prefers a white man

I am buried under the dirt of being fat
In a world that prefers slim

I am buried under the dirt of being single
In a world structured for couples

Seldom am I nourished with the water of significance
Or shined on by the sun

Yet I rise

I prayed that a simple pinch would not change the incredibility of this day
That all the euphoria I was feeling was completely genuine
America, the United States of America, had elected its first Black President
Barack Hussein Obama – from poverty to President
I wonder if his dad had known that he had fathered the 44th president of America
Would he have still walked away
Or would he have stayed to take part in creating the awesome man that often stands before us
with his family and promises hope, even without speaking
If a black man can be elected president, then a college dropout can earn a master's degree
If a black man can be elected president, then a single mother can purchase her first house in
which to raise her children
If a black man can be elected president, an overweight woman can meet and marry the man of
her dreams
Tomorrow's hopes are resurrected by today's achievements, in spite of yesterday's
misjudgments
I can do anything
You can do anything
In a country braided with money and power and laced with prejudice and racism, victory for
the underdog is still possible!
If God be for you, it matters not who stands against you
Make no mistake, this day was architectured by God
He knew when we were yet in the wilderness that he had a promised land waiting for us
Bush-wilderness, gas prices-wilderness, recession-wilderness, loss of jobs-wilderness, war-
wilderness
Barack Hussain Obama-promised land
Is he a miracle-working answer to all of America's problems?
Absolutely not!
He's simply the instrument used by God to level the field so that an overweight, single-mother
who dropped out of college, could once again have a glimmer of hope that it's possible for her
and her children to achieve
Everything they dream of
Everything they strive for

Test Drive

You wanna sleep with me because I'm sexy
And that's private
But you won't marry me because I'm fat
And that's public
But you can't walk into a car dealership to buy an engine
You have to purchase the whole car
So if all you want to do is pick your part
I suggest you lower your standards and troll the junkyard
But I am not junkyard material!

You see I was ranked best in quality and performance
By JB Power and Associates
The JB stands for Jesus' Blood
So, unless you are ready to make a serious offer
Then please move around, kick rocks, I don't know, whatever
Just make room for the one willing to make an investment
In something of value
Because he recognizes class when he sees it
And he wants to ensure that no one else
Drives me off that showroom floor but him

You see when you turned away
Because I wasn't much to look at from the outside
He took the time to check out the interior
So he knows that even though I ain't riding on dubs
My seats are soft and subtle top grain leather
My body may be super-sized
But my engine can take a lickin and keep on tickin
And I'm hood-rich
That means I'm intelligent
But what you're thinking is true as well!

Now am I saying I haven't foolishly given away my parts in the past
Or compromised myself by giving men discounts they didn't deserve
No!
But when I returned to the manufacturer
And begged Him to restore me
Jesus, the Bounty Hunter
Went out and repossessed all my parts
But God said
You can't put old wine into new wine skin
So He made all my parts like new

So do me a favor
If you ever find yourself contemplating
Whether or not you should just settle for me
Don't!
My quality far exceeds that of anything "settled for"
And if you are too blind, crippled, and crazy to see that
Then I refuse to let you test drive me!

Make Me a Virgin Again

Lord please
Make me a virgin again!
Make me a virgin again
So that I can once more feel the purity of the spirit that You placed inside of me
So that I can once again feel the unconditional love that only You have perfected
To endure past my idiosyncrasies

Please Lord, make me a virgin again
Make me a virgin again so that my heart erases the memory
Of being molested by negativity and raped by disappointment
That weighed so heavily on me that it crushed the one rib that defines me as a woman

I beg you Lord, please make me a virgin again
Make me a virgin again so that my wholeness is tight enough to provide immense pleasure
Upon entrance
So that when the application of pressure is forcing its way through my soul
That it is Your blood that covers the wounds inflicted by negligence

Make me a virgin again Lord
So that I may abort feelings of inadequacy and fear
When impregnated with new opportunities to live and to love

It is I Lord
Who freely traded my virginity
When solicited for false hopes of contentment and gratification
And it is I Lord
Who stands here begging you
Please, to make me a virgin - once again

When I Grow Up

When I grow up

I want to speak French and Spanish fluently
I want to take pictures brought to life in my home-based dark room
I want to praise dance in church on Sundays

When I grow up

I want to watch my daughter's little league games and cheerleader practices
I want to cross that stage to receive my degree
I want to marry the man of my dreams, damn what others think of him

When I grow up

I want to write poems that inspire people the way Maya, Nikki, Iyanla, and
        Ntozake inspired me
I want to travel unbeaten paths for single parents the way Barbara, Martin,
        Harriett, Thurgood, and Barack did for Black people
I want to fill my soul with performances by
        Dancers like Debbie, Judith, and Alvin
        Singers like Rachelle, Yolanda, Teena, India, Anita, Celine, and Lauren
                    Joe, Kenny, Luther, Tyrese, and Donny
        Musicians like Kenny G, Ben, Boney, Kirk, and Wynton
        Comedians like Ricky, Ced, Steve, Tiffany, Kevin, Katt and Loni
        Thespians like Larenz, Cuba, Leon, Denzel, Blair and Samuel,
                    Billy Jones and Donis Leonard (undiscovered but awesome)
                Nia, Cicely, Halle, Debbie, Angela, and Alfre
        Speakers of the truth like TD, Juanita, Eddie, and Kirbyjon

When I grow up

I want to make a difference in the lives of others by sharing
     My failures and triumphs
     My dreams and disappointments
     My fears and my faith

When I grow up, I want to be whole

Sent from Heaven

I prayed…
God, please, send me a man that loves me
Send me a man willing to navigate
Around the weaknesses of my flesh
That he may get lost in the strength of my spirit
A man that understands that I was born in imperfection
But purified by the fire of continued attempts to improve

The moment I saw him
I knew he had been sent by God
And I couldn't take my eyes off him
Tall, dark, and handsome
His skin had been kissed by chocolate
His eyes so wide
They reminded me of circles drawn by preschoolers
That they had colored outside the lines

And he used them
He used them to appreciate women
Of all shapes, shades, sizes, and financial statuses
Innocently he appreciated the essence of what God had created
And called woman
Often feeling compelled to elaborate on the beauty
He saw in them at that moment
You look beautiful today or
I like your hair like that he'd say
Satisfied that he had made his mark on her day

Imagine my surprise the first time he ran ahead of me
To hold the door, not only for me

But for all who entered behind me
Beaming with joy at every expression of gratitude

Thank you, Lord, I remember to say before I go to bed
Thank you for answered prayer
In whatever manifestation you choose to deliver it
He looks me in the eyes as he thanks God for me
And together, our communication with the Father ends with Amen

Though he lights up every time he sees me
I think he smiles his brightest when I wake him in the morning
But it disappears with any hint of sadness found in my eyes
I know he probably sounds perfect
He's not
But I'm continuously amazed by his growth
We could not have been
More perfect for each other
If I had gone to heaven and hand-picked him myself

He loves me
He truly loves me beyond anything I could have ever imagined
He lifts me when I am down
He greets me when I've been away
He seeks my advice for answers to life's questions

He also knows that when he wants something
He only has to look at me with those big beautiful eyes
And I melt like butter
Even if I've told him no a million times
Have I told you how much I love him
More than life itself
Which is why it pains me to remember
The one thing God forgot to tell me when he sent him

What do I tell him Lord when he asks me about his Father?

I Think He Wrote
(John 8:6-8)

My beautiful child
If only you would share your most intimate self with me
As you have with so many others
I could fill your emptiness with the bread of life
And the fountain of love

You would never hunger or thirst again
For resolution in a world
That simply has none to offer

Then He turned to her and said
Your sins are forgiven
Go and sin no more

The Very Essence of You

The very essence
Of fruit
Sweetness
The very essence
Of you
Not total perfection
But perfect none the less
For me, for you, for us

Remembering S. C.

There were many others present
They merely served as your background
Focus!
Oh these eyes betray me
They only see yours
So big, so bright, so full of awe
They obviously see something they like
And then—
I'm sorry did you say something?
You're a very attractive young lady
Did I say thank you?
I think I said thank you
I thought it
Just before my ears went numb
Refusing to relinquish your eloquent acclamation
Say something
Don't just sit there
He's leaving
What did I say?
I don't remember
It doesn't matter
In my hand a scrap of paper
Your phone number was simply titled *S. C.*

Essence II

A taste
Unlike any other
So sweet, so gentle, so strong
No judging
Simple, pure
Unconditional savor

All That I Am

I am beautiful
Because you gave me beauty

I am strong
Because you gave me strength

I am loved
Because you gave me love

I live
Because you gave me life

All that I am
I am because of you

While I Wait

What am I supposed to do
While I'm waiting to be found
While the man whose rib I carry
 Is still out there playing around

His buddies tell him he's still young
So he's frolicking from pillow to post
And while he may not be sleeping with all of 'em
I'll bet you he's sleeping with most

Oh you can sit there and act like what I'm saying ain't true
I can't tell you what to believe
But one thing I know for certain
Those kids weren't immaculately conceived

What am I supposed to do
Just sit here and wait
20...30...40...50
Hell, it's almost too late

Look, I don't know what you're doing
And I surely don't know where you're at
I don't know if you just can't see perfection
Cause it's buried underneath a little fat

But if you knew there was a million dollars
Buried underneath a big old tree
Raise your hand if you wouldn't go dig for it
Well apply that same principal to me

What am I supposed to do
While you go on with your life
I'll tell you what I'm gonna do
I'm gonna prepare myself to be your wife

While I wait for you, I'll be praying
That God blesses you with undeniable favor
And as he impregnates you with life-changing possibilities
Know that I'll stand beside you and support you as you labor

Then I'll just keep waiting on God
To allow our paths to cross
But if you let me walk out of your life at that time
Well, that will be your loss

But still, what's a girl to do
While she's waiting on the Lord
How about learn the difference between
A running back, a quarter back, and a point guard

And know that even then, I should get out of the way occasionally
And leave the big screen for you and your boys to watch the game
But just remember when it's girl's night
Your commitment to my "Me Time" has got to be the same

What am I supposed to do
When my man won't come out of my dreams
Well, they say a good meal is the way to a man's heart
And it wouldn't hurt to keep my house clean

And yes, I know for those of you who have children
That's not always easy to do
But ah…ah…ah…treat those kids with kindness
Cause he needs to know that you'll take good care of *his* kids, too

What am I supposed to do
While I wait on that heaven-sent day
Become that Proverbs 31 Woman
So that Jezebel can't steer you away

And finally, while I wait for you my king
I'll tackle my toughest feat
And that's to make sure that ten years down the line
I'm just as sexy as I am on the day we finally meet

Your Special Gift

Thank you, Father
For your special gift
More beautiful than the setting sun
More precious than a priceless jewel
Living proof of your faith in me
When I had none in myself

I can't imagine
Loving anyone more
She claims every fiber of my heart
Not reserved for You
My only wish
To please her
In accordance with Your will
Make her proud that she is mine
And I am hers

She is the best parts of me
In their own little package
So I wish to protect her
Take her hand in mine
Guide her through life's ups and downs
That she always comes out on top
Making it easier for her to look to You

If she stumbles
I want to be there
Always be there
For as long as she needs me
To pick her up, dust her off

Start her back on her way

Walk with me Father
As I travel this road
Hold me
When I am too weary to hold myself
Give me strength
To be Your vessel as
Mother of my beautiful daughter

Black Woman

Black Woman

Black Woman

When will you learn

Of all the respect

That you have earned

Let it show through your smile

Your verse and your step

Speak with assurance

Walk with some pep

Go through the motions

Keep heads spinning

Politely inform

That it's just the beginning

Your gift is sufficient

It comes from God, not from man

But now, how you use it

Is all in your hands

You go girl!

Just strut your stuff

And you let them know

When "enough is enough"

Hats

The dictionary defines a hat as a covering for the head
Or a fashion accessory
But in truth for most women
A hat is more a statement of responsibility
You see our hats tell the story
Of what work needs to be done
And as a woman
I'm never able to wear just one

I wear a hat cuz I'm a mother
So I must cook and clean
But mothers are also doctors, cab drivers, judge and jury,
Homework helpers, motivational speakers
The end of this list is unseen

I wear a hat cuz I'm a wife
And my husband's needs must be met
But sometimes when I'm in need of nourishment
My husband tends to forget

I wear a hat cuz I'm a girlfriend
And if I don't meet my man's expectations, he'll walk away
But at times I've given all I've had
And still that didn't convince him to stay

I wear a hat cuz I'm a pastor
And my sheep have to be led
And even when they're the ones who've emptied the cupboard
My sheep still expect to be fed

I wear a hat cuz I'm a child of God
And he expects my best
So that even if you come to me broken
You should leave me blessed

Sisters let me encourage you
To wear your hats with pride
And if one of those hats gets too heavy
Then just cock it to the side

But if all your hats get too heavy
And you feel yourself wearing down
Stand tall Queen
Cuz someday God will take all those hats
And exchange them for your crown

A Million Men

O great day
You've finally come
We've traveled the world
To unite as one
No song has been sung
No story's been told
That could've prepared us
For what this day would unfold
Thousands spoke against it
Hundreds finally came around
Still nearly two million
Stood strong on the ground

O great day
You're finally here
To heal all our children
And wipe our mothers' tears
Our leaders are learning
Of the problems we face
In my heart I feel a change
Is about to take place
They're coming to save us
Come one and come all
To end cries of "Save me,
Please don't let me fall"

O great is the day
When we can rejoice
To see our men listening
To one single voice

And pledging correction
For the wrong in their lives
To reclaim their children
And uplift their wives
To love all brothers
As they love their own
To realize that sisters
Belong on a throne
For they are all queens
Not Bitches as said
And thank God in Heaven
That myth is now dead
They're pledging to stop
The drugs and the death
To not be responsible
For someone's last breath

O glory to God
For it is only he
Who could bring about the changes
That we're about to see
Oh yes there is no doubt
The changes are near
Just look toward heaven
And there's no need to fear
Rise up people
Let's all join hands
The war is ending
All over the land
The stars are dancing
For even they see
The splendor forthcoming
In a world of unity

The Prodigal Son

Love is patient
Love is kind
For he who loves
It's also blind

To imperfections
Large and small
Sure to exist within us all

To love
You must set angels free
To loose the chains
Of uncertainty

A father's love
One can be sure
Waits patiently
Behind eternity's door

For the Prodigal son
Whose sins are so great
They create a grave
For his royalty trait

So amongst filth and swine
He makes himself known
Until heaven's reminder
Guides him back home

He does not travel far
To meet his father's waiting arms
And receive exoneration
From self-inflicted harm

But how can you accept me, he asks
As dirty as I am
My son because you're covered
In the blood of the Holy Lamb

So, forgiveness is not an option
It's mandated from above
We're called to focus not on shortcomings
But on God's demonstration of love
You see the father in the story
Represents God at His best
And the wayward son that Luke speaks of
Is us in the midst of our mess

Like the Prodigal son
Our sins are much too great to bear
But wherever it is they break us down
God will meet us there

His love is unconditional
No matter what we've done
A fatted calf awaits the return
Of all God's daughters and sons

The robe and crown are yours as well
When you take your rightful place
Don't worry about tomorrow
It's covered by His grace

Don't fret of over your shortcomings
For one thing I have learned
Redemption is a gift from God
It simply can't be earned

What I Need You For

I am an intelligent, strong, independent Black Woman

I'm told I intimidate men

Why? Because…

I don't need your car, I drive a Lexus

I don't need your house, I have a home

I don't need your job, I have a career

I don't need your money, I have God's favor

So, what I need you for?

I need to see your face light up when I enter a room

I need you to let me be right, *MOST* of the time

I need you to complete my sentences

I need you to reassure me that everything is gonna be alright, cuz you got me!

I need you to undress me

I need you to devour the meals I prepare for you like they are your last

I need you to work on my "Honey Do" list

I need you to look at me like I'm the most beautiful thing in the world (even when I look a mess)

I need you to touch me

I need you to treat me like I am the queen that I am

I need you to talk me out of making bad decisions

I need you to already have all the kids you want! And I need you to love mine.

I need you to protect me

I need you to bless me with small surprises…just because

I need you to blow my back out!

I need your buddies to know how much you love me without you saying a word

I need you slide me a few dollars, not because I need it, but because I deserve it

When you go out with your boys and this chick walks in with a body so banging, all of you look at her and simultaneously say, "DAMN!"

I need you to come home and take every inch of that out on me…I digress!

I need you to pray for me

When I am wrong as hell, I need you to have my back anyway
I need you to want to spend time with me, even when you can't
I need you to tell me _and_ show me how you feel about me
I need you to not only show me respect, but ensure others do as well
I need us to build a life _together_
What I need you for?
In short, I need you to love me

There Is No Place I'd Rather Be

There is no place on earth I'd rather be
Then nestled in the folds of God's natural beauty
Warmed by the radiance of His Son
Comforted by the angels of Grace and Mercy
There is no milk and honey here…no streets paved in silver and gold
Only atmospheric flirtations like the kiss of the sun and the warmth of the wind
That wraps itself around me

God's essence saturates the air negating vacancies until there is no room left for weaknesses
-Or strengths
They don't matter here, only Him
The birds translate His love notes into melodic scores of His affection
If I am quiet, I can hear the flowers bloom, gaining life at His command
In the distance, the tranquil sounds of the ocean keep time
In an effort to slow the pace of my thoughts
The rain, like baby's breath taps ever so gently on my soul
To Finesse away the stresses of the day

There's no place I'd rather be
Then captured in the ambiance of my Father's unfailing love
His kind and gentle spirit nudges me past fear and uncertainty
To savor the aroma of victory over life's trials and tribulation
I am consistently amazed by the combination of qualities He has displayed before my eyes
My pupils dance in appreciation of the colorful hues of the rainbow that He set
Just as a simple reminder of His adoration for me

The mountains serve as a memento that there will be ups and downs through the
Labyrinth of life
But He promised me a comforter

The gift of His agape love, like fine China, should be handled with the utmost care
Yet it is neither fragile nor breakable

There is no place I'd rather be
Then in the whisper of my Maker's wisdom
In hopes that His reflection is evident in every demonstration
Of His influence over my life
I am but an embryo
Depending solely on Him for survival
I need him like a pen needs her poet
At day's end, my hope is that He would crown me with but a morsel of His glory
Declare before me, well done, my good and faithful servant
And grant that I may ever here after abide in Him and Him in me
Because when all is said and done
There is absolutely, positively no other place I'd rather be

Reflections

She faces the mirror
The reflection is of myself
My spirit, my values, my needs surface

I'm overwhelmed by the realization
That so much of me
Lives and breathes inside of her

She is so beautiful
An angel she seems
A gift from heaven
Every mother's dream

Thank you, Lord, for allowing me to see
The God in her
That she received through me

Thank you that even though I'm not perfect
I have helped to fill her spirit with righteousness
And a genuine love for you, for herself, and for others

Thank you for your affirmation of love

I Wondered...

I stood stoically and watched as she
Leaped and clapped in unison with the
Rhythmic vibrations of the timekeeper's drum
Yes, I told myself it was rude to stare
But numerous attempts to avert my gaze
Proved futile at best

Her smile took me hostage as I found myself
Deliberating the possibilities of catastrophes
Responsible for the distortion of her face
Her skin had been left in a mangled collage of flesh
That no doubt some doctor had
Optimized several opportunities to restore

I wondered

Had she crawled on her knees
Across a maple-colored floor
Screaming for someone, anyone to help her, save her
Had she earnestly tried to escape
A torrent of flames that carelessly tore patches of skin
From the skeletal foundation that formed her face
Had she beckoned for God
Praying that some way, somehow the ranks of tears
Parading down her cheeks would miraculously subdue the fire
Just long enough for her to prevail
Had she been hindered because every new attempt to breathe fresh air
Left her more asphyxiated by swirling billows of smoke

I wondered

Why was she there
Had the tall, lanky teen standing lovingly beside her
Been the one in danger
Had she fearlessly negated all attempts
By the blistering blaze to claim the life of her only child
Had her perseverance pilgrimed her to a point of no return

I wondered

Or had some angry, jealous, out of control partner
Stolen her beauty
Had he been so determined to retard any social advances
That challenged his predatory engagement
That he allowed the situation to escalate to a height
That demanded the projectile dashing of acid into her face
Had the combination of both the physical pain and the emotional pain
Been so excruciating that even her heart-wrenching screams
Proved inadequate in her search
For the most minute measure of comfort

I wondered

How much time had carefully positioned itself on the dash
Between her yesterdays and her tomorrows
And what had taken her from that desperate place of agony and despair
To this peaceful paradox in which she presently dwells

Jesus

With every repetitious announcement of His name, in song
She leaped higher and higher
As if being propelled further and further from the ailing cataclysms of her past

I watched as the tempo of her claps accelerated
Her hands danced in celebration of the reality that
The joy of God was now the aggressor to which she gratefully fell victim

I wondered

If something similar had happened to me
Could I stand in His presence
Smiling, clapping, leaping
Thankful for life

I wondered

Now I Know

Now I know how my mom must have felt when my dad left
How when I was fast asleep, she spent many nights crying alone
Because she refused to let her children see her shed seemingly endless tears
And no one else knew the pain she was in

Now I know how empty her bed must have felt and how empty her heart was
When she finally gave up on the love she realized could never be what she needed
Now I know why she must've worked so much to keep her mind busy
Because the devil wreaks havoc on an idle mind and an empty heart

Now I know how she waited for time to take away the hurt consuming her
How she felt abandoned, even by God
How both the days and nights seemed too long
How miniscule, irrelevant, and unloved she felt

Now I know how it feels to never want to cry again
Never want to hurt again, never want to love again

Up to Here Widdit

I would like to give honor to God
Who will bless you with a gift
And fill you up to here widdit

Then He will pass the baton to you
So that you can run the last leg
And it's up to you to gain the victory

Remembering that no matter
How many times you stumble
How many times you drop the baton
How many times you forget to thank Him
For bringing you this far

He is always near to pick you up
Dust you off
And place you back on solid foundation

I love you Father
Thank you for your Grace
And for blessing us with a gift
And filling us up to here widdit

Too Much to Ask

Why do you assume I'm insecure when I ask you "how do I look?" or "how was the food?"
I'm not asking because I need you to validate me
I know that I am beautiful, I don't doubt my sexiness
And I am convinced that I am an amazing woman
Nothing you say (or don't say) will change that
Because If I gave you the power to build me up
I would also be giving you the power to tear me down
I am not willing to do that
I'm asking because I want to know what *you* think, what *you* feel
I want you to trust me with your inner thoughts and feelings
I need you to know that I will not use them against you
Almost every day, *someone* tells me how nice I look and yes, it feels great
But not as good as it would feel if it were coming from you
If you don't find me attractive, sexy, or amazing, that's fine
But then, why are you here?
If you do, then every now and then, why not just tell me?
Not every minute of every day or every day of every week
But just enough to remind me that I am a woman
That you are a man that appreciates the woman I am
And that you are with me because there is no one else on earth with whom you'd rather be
Is that too much to ask?

Bruised but Not Broken

God has given me a spiritual gift
That I must use to provide a spiritual lift
And sometimes I'm awakened at a ghastly hour
Just so He can explain to me how to help you re-claim your power

So if you're here today and you're wounded
God has sent you a token
He has commissioned me to remind you
That you're bruised, but not broken

He's says don't forget
What He said in his word
Your path He will light
Your loins He will gird

So when darts are coming at you
From north, south, east, and west
Remember, He says
It's only a test

Cause no weapon formed against you
Will prosper, indeed
For you, child of God
Are Abraham's seed

So if in financial peril
It seems you are chokin'
God says just remember
You're bruised, but not broken

For all things belong to Him
Say it with me "All things"
Not just a few
And if His eye is on the tiny sparrow
How much more is His mind on you

He says ask and you shall receive
Seek and you shall find
Knock and the door shall be opened
Remember in all things
You are bruised, but not broken

Now, for those who have lost someone
And you feel your heart can't bear it
God says lay your burden on the altar
And He will gladly share it

For he knows what it's like to pour out so much love
Yet not feel love return
Think about it, He gave his son for us
Yet for our love He still must yearn

To those of you waiting for something
That seems it will never come to pass
God says remember He's Alpha and Omega
And His word is the First and the Last

I pray that you've been blessed by something I've said
Or even healed by something I've spoken
But even if nothing you've heard has touched your heart
Please, just remember, you're bruised, but not broken

Seems like my whole life
I've been haunted by the same three words
In Your Season
Friends, Family, Pastors, and Strangers
Have all made the same promise for forty years
In Your Season

During these years I've lost my Dad
Not to death, but to divorce
Because when he left my mom
He thought that meant he had to leave me too but
In Your Season

Within these years I was molested
By someone who was supposed to protect me but
In Your Season

Amid these years I fell in love
And gave my mind, heart, and body
To men who swore they loved me
Yet time after time
I found myself alone
Each time more alone than the last but
In Your Season

In the midst of these years
I worked a job with no appreciation
No promotion
And little compensation but
In Your Season

Throughout these years
I've had to raise my children alone
Struggling to keep a roof over our heads
Clothes on our backs
Food on our table but
In Your Season

With the passing of these years
I watched as others were blessed
With spouses, houses, careers
Nice cars, vacations, extensive wardrobes
Businesses and miracles from God
The promise has always been the same
In Your Season

Well if you are here today
And like me you can no longer bear to hear
One more person say those three words again
In Your Season
I have four new words for you
Your Season is Now!

This is your season
This is your day
This is the time for things
To start going your way

The time has come
For you to stand
In all the things
That God has planned

You've remained faithful
Through so many things
Now's the time to enjoy
The blessings Your Season brings

Know that things won't be easy
For the devil knows what's to come
But when he wages his war against you
Know that you've already won
Your Season is Now

Walk into God's promises
Let no one hold you back

Press toward the mark of the higher calling
Call forth everything you lack

God says it's yours
For you are heir to His throne
And even when you thought you were forsaken
God says He counted every groan
Your Season is Now

For you the struggle is over
Reach up and get your crown
And to the next person that promises
In Your Season
You tell them
My Season is Now!

The truth is
Some Men, especially black men
Don't believe that strong, black women deserve love
They think since we decided to survive in their absence
Then that's what we should do for the rest of our lives

So they use us
They use us for their own self-indulgences
And then they justify it by telling themselves that we are strong,
We can handle it
And they proceed to do the same thing over and over and over again
Until they are bored

Then they set their sights on women of other races
Or black women that don't "look" or "act" black
But instead appear to belong to other races
Because they are easier to deal with
Leaving behind masses of children
Who don't understand why they weren't enough
For daddy to stay

Those that fail to conquer the hearts
Of those kinds of women
Become bitter towards all black women
Because the rest of us are invisible to them anyway
They start dogging out all black women
Even the ones that have tried to do nothing but love them
From the beginning
If that isn't enough
Some men have the audacity to blame black women for choosing "bad" men
As if they presented themselves that way

No, I am not bitter
I am a strong black woman
And I am proud to stand and shine
Even if I do so without you

Where Do I Sign

There are so many things that take place in this vast world
Evil things, things that hurt
Things that can make you wish you'd never been born
It is so hard to see, so hard to hear about
The travesties that plague this nation, this world
Innocent men and women
Who just needed to pay for college
Are losing their lives in a foreign land
Children are not safe in school
Parents are not safe at home
Men are finding more pleasure in children
Then they are in women
Women are finding more comfort in drugs
Then in their families
Sex, money, and power have become the top aspirations
Instead of Love, Health, and Salvation
Men are sleeping with men
Women are marrying women
Babies are having babies
While grown folk are denied the chance
And if crippling and tragic diseases aren't enough
Senseless killings afflict our homes, our nation, our world
Divorce is rampant
Couples that once loved each other so much they couldn't see straight
Are clear about the hatred that has obliterated their relationship
Others can't find love to save their lives
There are so many things that take place in this vast world
Evil things, things that hurt
Things that make you wish you'd never been born
But in the grand scope of things
There is One
One that can give you peace that surpasses all understanding
One that can show you that even with everything going on around you
With everything going on inside of you
You were created for a divine purpose

You are here to make a difference in this world
And in the lives of others
In the end you will reap what you have sown
I know that God will never leave us or forsake us
So, if given the choice between bearing my cross or not
I say, Where Do I Sign?

So...

You need a woman who can stand beside you and support you in achieving your goals and dreams for yourself, for your family

I can do that

You need a woman who can massage every area of your body until tension has no place to hide

I can do that

You need a woman who can be down with you no matter how crazy that crap you saying sounds

I can do that

You need a woman who can cook and serve your dinner, run your bath water, and sing you to sleep after a hard day's work

I can do that (*just not every day*)

You need a woman who can wake you up in the middle of the night just to give you that gift you like so much, just the way you like it

I can do that

You need a woman who can love and care for your children as if they passed through her own womb

I can do that

You need a woman who knows just what to say and do just when you need it because she listens more than she talks

I can do that

You need a woman who can't hide her feelings for you because she lights up every time you enter a room

I can do that

You need a woman who can not only be strong when you're weak, but can be weak when you're strong

I can do that

You need a woman who can give you her undivided attention when you have something you just gotta get off your chest

I can do that

You need a woman who can help keep you sane in the daytime, but make you lose your mind at night

I can do that

You need a woman who can appreciate the times when tears are the only way to release the heaviness on your heart

I can do that

You need a woman who can pray you out of a situation you know in your heart you had no business getting yourself into in the first place

I can do that

You need a woman who can encourage you and help you see that losing your job is just an opportunity for God to bless you rather that telling you how long your lazy tail got to find another one

I can do that

You need a woman who can be so good to you that, like your cell phone, you can't remember how you ever lived without her

I can do that

You need a woman who can make you feel so much like a man that you go and get a big S tatted on your chest, tie a bed sheet around your neck, and stand over the bed talkin' bout *"dot dah dah dah"*

I can do that

You need a woman who can hold you so tight, you feel completely safe from all the darts the world throws at you

I can do that

You need a woman who you cannot imagine spending one more day of your life without

I can do that

Yes, I can be your *whole* in One

The question is, can you be mine?

Masterpiece

The one thing I've wanted most in life
Is the one thing even to this day
That continues to escape me
But I refuse to let it shape me
I refuse to let it break me
And I refuse to allow the absence of it to take me
I yearned for it as a little girl
I long for it as woman
It would be so easy to blame my dad
I don't
How do you blame a parent
For not providing something
They simply didn't have to give
How could he keep me from getting lost
When he was still trying to find himself
So I pressed on
Looking forward to the day when a man
Thee man would pick up what he dropped
But instead I was violated, molested
By a man who saw all the broken pieces
And thought she's already broken
How much more damage can I do
I was thirteen when he used me to fulfill his lustful desires
I began to think he was doing me a favor
So I began to create opportunities for him to molest me
Eventually both my mind and body
Grew strong enough to fight him
But I was no match for the high school boys
That teased and ridiculed me
Or played with my heart and left me to die
But I live
There are holes within me that may never be filled
But I stand
I stand for what's right and what's good
So surely something good will come to me

Life will provide everything I missed growing up
52 years have passed
Year after year I've revived and replenished the hope
Of simply being loved and supported by a man
One man
That I can lean on when I get weak
That I can turn to when I need help
That I can depend on when I need advice
One man
That can look at the shattered pieces
And still fall in love with a
Masterpiece

The Second Woman

How could you be so perfect for me
Yet spend your life with someone else
Does she know my heart beats for you
Can she look into my eyes and see you in my soul

For the first time in my life
I want to be someone else
I long to be her
Because she is loved by you, touched by you, completed by you

Tell me, does she laugh at your jokes the way I do
Or appreciate the dance of your voice's vibrato
When your funny bone is fondled
Can she complete your sentences?

Never mind, don't answer that
I'm aware this line of questioning is unfair
But so is letting go of the only man that
Touches me like the wind
Warms me like the sun
And quenches me like water
I've loved you for so long
I don't remember what not loving you feels like
Yet it was her heart that reaped the harvest
That my sincerity sowed
I remind myself often that God is in control
And that everything that is, is supposed to be
In my head it all makes perfect sense
But I can't convince my heart
That we weren't meant for each other, made for each other

Most days I'm ecstatically happy for you
Convinced your marriage will last a lifetime
Then there are days like today
When all I want is for you to run back to my waiting arms

Declaring the realization that you cannot live another day – without me

I know what you're thinking…that is just plain wrong
But so is letting go of the only man that
Touches me like the wind
Warms me like the sun
And quenches me like water

Hell, he was mine first anyway
We just needed a little time
The one thing we didn't have apparently
But what I do have
Is a decision to make
Because in my heart I know that time heals all wounds
But distance is the antibiotic
So, which is harder
Not having you in my heart
Or not having you in my life
I've already been forced to give up
My hopes, my dreams, my future with you

Is separation the only tourniquet
That can stop the flow of love
That leaves my heart
Every time we speak
Every time we meet
Or is perseverance the solution
To push past the pain like a pregnant woman
Diligent to deliver the new gift that God has given
Wait…
That's the answer!

In 1 Kings, Chapter 3, verses 16-27
God's word speaks of two women
Both declaring motherhood over one baby
Whey they bring the issue to the king for a ruling
He calls for his sword that he may cut the baby in two
And give them each half

The first woman hastily agrees
Thankful for a resolution
The second woman, filled with compassion for the baby says
No, do not kill him; give the living baby to the other woman
For she could not bear to see him hurt
I, too, know what I must do

My True Worth

If my true worth is what you're hoping to find
My social security number should be the last thing that comes to mind
Those nine numbers given to me by "the man"
Are nothing more than a façade masking God's divine plan
They can't tell you that I'm a fourth-generation single mother
Surviving with what little help I get
Or that even with no support from their fathers
All of my children's needs have been met
My social security number doesn't tell you I'm up early every morning
Thanking God for one more day
Asking him for traveling mercy as I go to work
In spite of how little they pay
Those nine numbers hide the fact that people I trained are promoted ahead of me
Simply because of the color of my skin
Yet when something goes wrong with the process
It's this black face they're looking in
My social security number doesn't say that 10% of my earnings
Are returned to God as required, by way of the church
In return he stretches the other 90%
Far beyond what it's really worth
It only suggests to you that I can't be trusted
Because I struggle to pay my bills
So instead you put all your faith in the person that can *show you the money*
Never mind that it came from daddy's will
If my true worth is what you're hoping to find
My social security number is the last thing that should be on your mind
Because even though my liabilities outweigh my assets
Anything worth having is worth working for and waiting for, so I have no regrets
No, those nine numbers don't praise me
For giving college a second chance
Or for passing up overtime at work
Because I made a commitment to praise dance
Instead they try hard to convince both you and me
That I am not truly a Queen

Because right now I'm struggling down the pathway
That leads to all of my dreams
My social security number may identify me to you
But it doesn't make me question who I am
I know I'm a God-fearing, more-than-a-conqueror child of God
So go tell that to Uncle Sam
Aah yes, the American Dream...to own your own home
Guaranteed to make your money appreciate
But because those numbers tell you I'm not worth it
Me and my children must wait?
Does it say anywhere that my rent is paid monthly
And paid in a timely manner
No that's right only the things I do wrong
Are displayed on that national banner
I'm thankful God doesn't use my social security number
To decide what my future will be
His report says what I have for you is for you
So I could care less what they see
Because I was raised by a strong black woman
And she raised me to be one as well
She said Baby even when negative things happen
You should have a positive story to tell
So I'll leave you with this, God had a plan for you
Before you were placed on this earth
And when He created you, He deposited so much value into you
That nothing man ever devises could determine how much you're truly worth

If Only You Knew

If only you knew
The joy I felt when I realized God had blessed me with you
Oh I was scared as hell
If Laura Francis was your mother, you would've been scared too!
But deep inside,
A glimmer of hope could be found tucked inside that blanket of fear
Because for the first time in my life
I had no doubt that it would matter that I was here
July 19th, 1989
The day my doctor promised me that I would get to meet you
But after 2 inductions and 13 hours of labor pain
You simply refused to be told what to do!
On July 31, the doctor finally decided
He would not be punked by no girl
So he put his foot down, picked his scalpel up,
And introduced you to the world
Besides asking God for a healthy baby girl
There was one other thing I'd prayed about
I begged God to please let you be beautiful
But never specified inside or out
He understood that I'd been hurt so much because of my external appearance
That as your Mother, I just didn't want that for you
God granted my desire and in spite of the fact that I did not appreciate His gift of internal beauty,
He went on and threw that in too
So...I had prayed for you to be a girl, to be healthy, and for you to be beautiful
I did not pray for you to be 6 feet tall.
But every gift God has given me through you, I embrace and cherish them all.
You may look just like your daddy,
But just like your mama, you are beautiful, gifted, intelligent, strong, kind and yes...at times, Loud
But that's a good thing because today I stand here as your mother, screaming!!!
"Of you, I could not be more proud!"

The Gift of Life

The most precious gift I have ever been given
Is the gift of life
For life represents God's continued faith in me
At times
This earth suit only seems to constrict the power of the spirit
God placed in me
But it is at those times
God whispers his promises of victory in my ear
It is then that He assures me
That if I just hold on
His every commitment, His every covenant
Will be manifested in my life
When I remind Him of my pain, He reminds me of His love
When I remind Him of my fear, He reminds me of His power
When I remind Him of my sin, He reminds me of His grace
So Lord
For every challenge You've turned into opportunity
For every valley You've turned into victory
For every stronghold You've allowed me to conquer
Lord, I thank You for my life